UNDERSTAND YOUR Mind AND Body

Autism

AJ Knight

Explore other books at:
WWW.ENGAGEBOOKS.COM

VANCOUVER, B.C.

WWW.ENGAGEBOOKS.COM

Know Your Mind - Depression: Level 3
Lee, Ashley 1995 –
Text © 2023 Engage Books
Design © 2023 Engage Books

Edited by: A.R. Roumanis and Sarah Harvey
Design by: Rose Gowsell Pattison
Consultant: Heather Romero - *Child Youth and Family Counsellor*

Text set in Arial Regular.
Chapter headings set in Arial Black.

This book is not meant to replace the advice of a medical professional or be a tool for diagnosis. It is an educational tool to help children understand what they or other people are going through.

FIRST EDITION / FIRST PRINTING

Photo of Armani Williams by Zach Catanzareti. Every reasonable effort has been made to contact the copyright holders of all material reproduced in this book.

LIBRARY AND ARCHIVES CANADA CATALOGUING IN PUBLICATION

Title: Autism: Understand Your Mind and Body Level 3 reader / AJ Knight
Names: Knight, Alyssa J, 1995- author

Identifiers: Canadiana (print) 20200308874 | Canadiana (ebook) 20200308912
ISBN 978-1-77476-776-4 (hardcover)
ISBN 978-1-77476-777-1 (softcover)
ISBN 978-1-77476-779-5 (pdf)
ISBN 978-1-77476-778-8 (epub)
ISBN 978-1-77878-104-9 (audio)

Subjects:
LCSH: Autism—Juvenile literature.
LCSH: Autism in children—Juvenile literature.

Classification: LCC BF723.A4 J66 2023 | DDC J152.4/7—DC23

This project has been made possible in part by the Government of Canada.

Canada

Contents

Autism is not an illness or a disease. Anyone can be autistic.

What is Autism?

Autism affects the brain. Autistic people communicate, socialize, and think differently than non-autistics. Autism is also called Autism Spectrum Disorder (ASD).

Using words like **high or low functioning** can be harmful and not accurate. Talking about the kind of support a person needs is more helpful. For example, some people need help in a big crowd.

KEY WORD

High or low functioning: an outdated way to explain how much help an autistic person needs.

Being 'on the autism spectrum' means that autism is different for each person.

What Causes Autism?

Autistic people are born with it. Signs of autism can be noticed before age three. Nothing is wrong with autistic people.

Autism may be passed down from your parents.

Each autistic person is unique. Autistic people will always have autism. Being autistic is just another way to exist as a person.

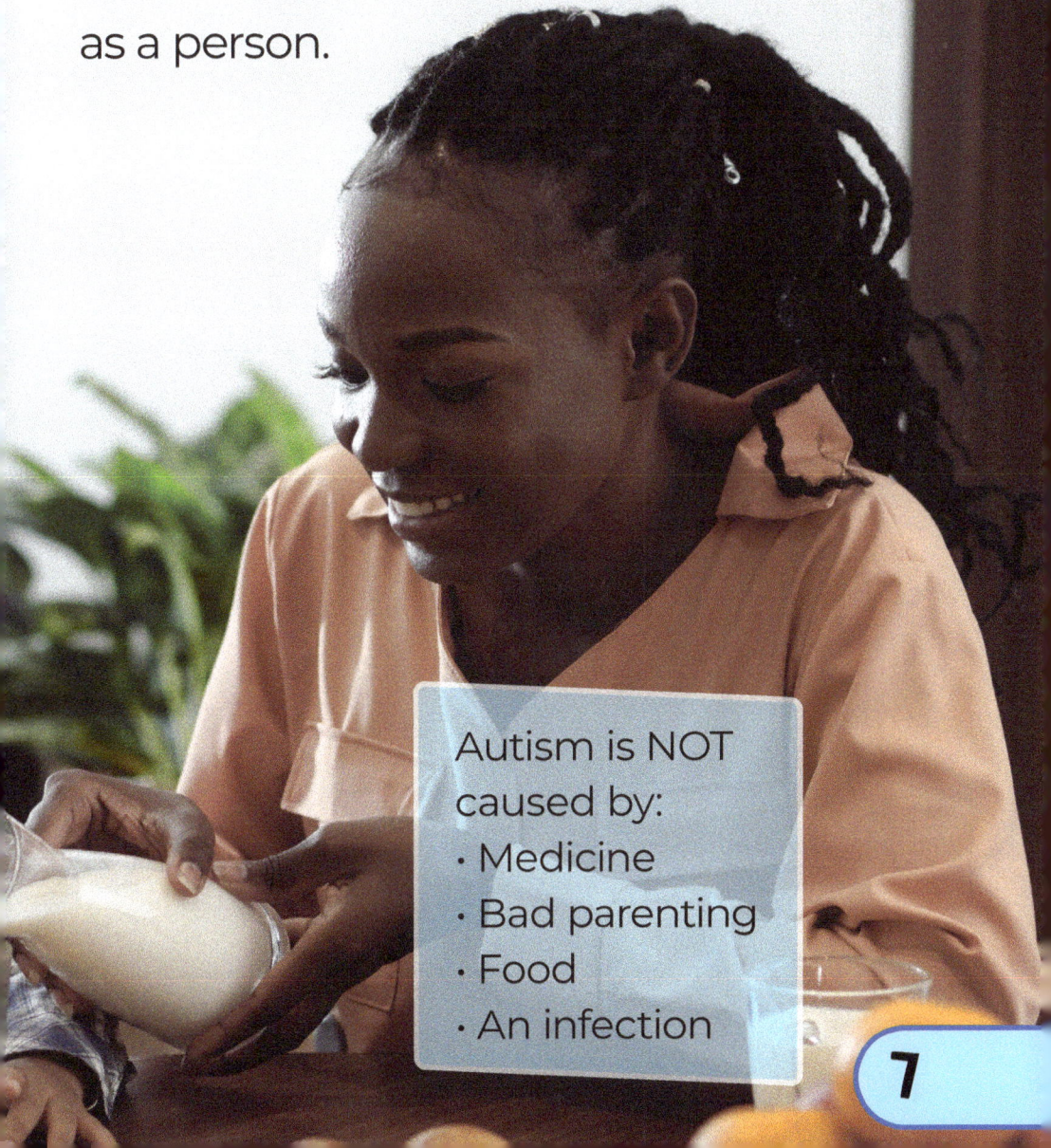

Autism is NOT caused by:
· Medicine
· Bad parenting
· Food
· An infection

How Does Autism Affect Your Brain?

Autistic brains can be bigger and heavier than non-autistic brains. Some parts of the brain have more connections. Other parts of the brain have fewer connections.

Autistic brains are about 3 percent larger than non-autistic brains.

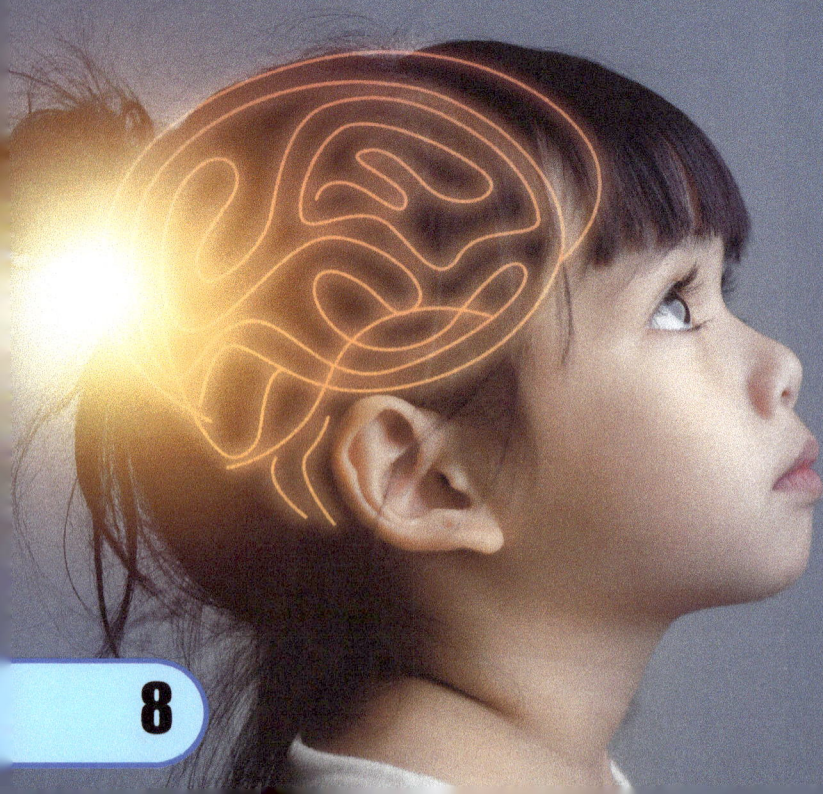

The **cerebrum** and **cerebellum** are different in autistic people. Autistic people may stand or move differently than non-autistics. Children with Autism usually have less control of their ankles, knees, and hips.

Cerebrum:

Part of the brain that helps us think, move, and understand language.

Cerebellum:

Part of the brain that helps us speak and control movement.

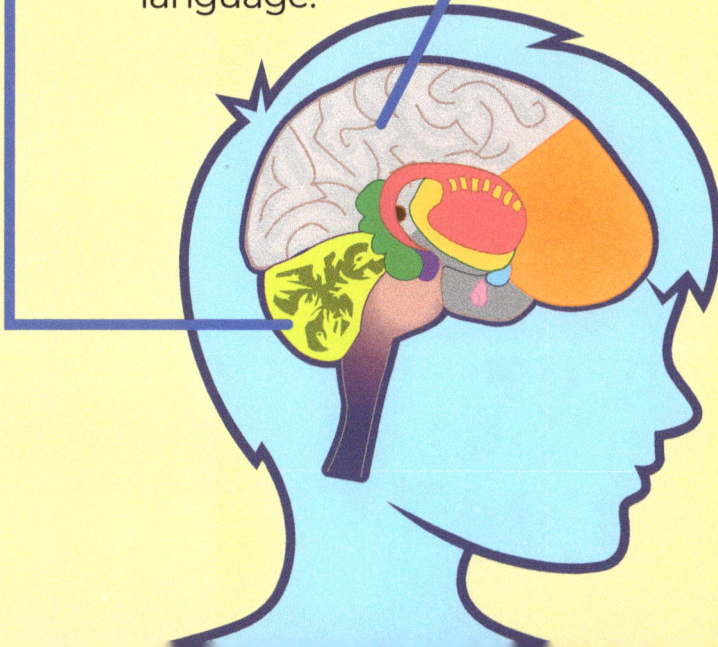

How Does Autism Affect Your Body?

Autistic babies can take longer to start walking and talking. Some autistics may walk on their tip toes or slouch. **Stimming** is common among autistics.

KEY WORD

Stimming: making repeated movements or sounds to stay calm or focused.

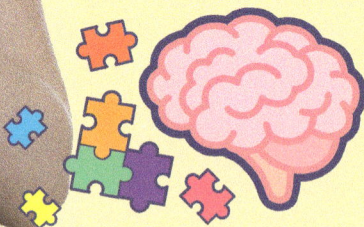

Some autistics have stronger senses than non-autistics. Loud noises, crowds, or scratchy clothes can feel very good or very bad. Some autistic people may be **non-verbal**.

KEY WORD

Non-verbal: unable to communicate by talking.

There are things you can do if you are overwhelmed. This includes stimming, and wearing headphones or sunglasses.

What Does Having Autism Feel Like?

Many autistic people say they feel different from everyone else. They might notice things that no one else does. Autistics often have **special interests**.

KEY WORD

Special interests: things you want to know everything about and can focus on forever.

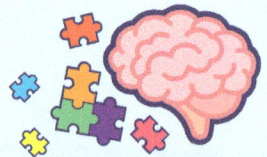

Many autistics say they feel like an alien compared to others.

Stress can cause meltdowns or shutdowns. A meltdown is when you get angry or upset. A shutdown is when you go quiet.

How Is Autism Diagnosed?

Doctors and **psychologists** can help people of any age figure out if they are autistic. They will ask you lots of questions about your life and how you feel and think about things.

KEY WORD

Psychologists: trained professionals who help people understand and change their behavior.

Sometimes symptoms of autism are not noticed. People do not get the help they need. Girls with autism are more likely to use **masking** in order to blend in.

KEY WORD

Masking: hiding behaviors that may set you apart from others.

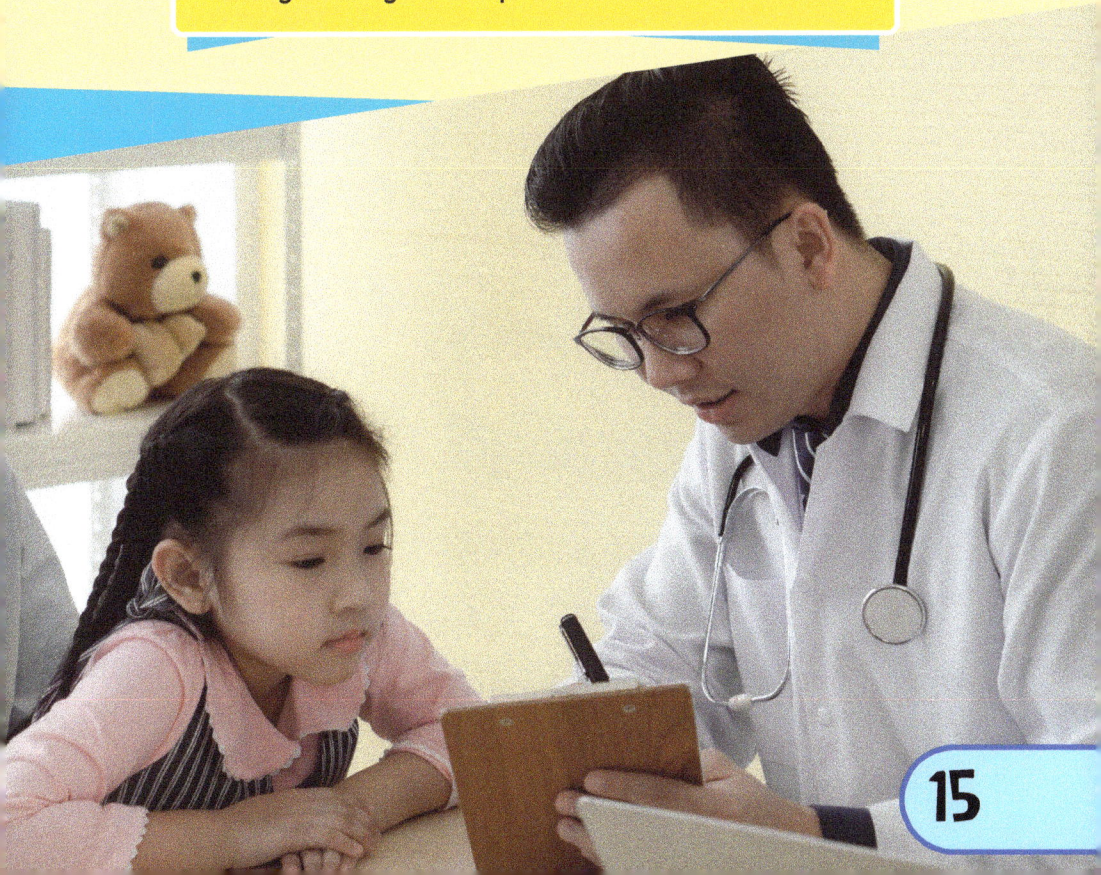

Asking For Help

Autistic people live in a world built for non-autistics. Think about how you best communicate with others. Asking for help may look different for each autistic person.

Asking for help can be difficult. But it is very important! Find an adult you can connect with about how you feel.

"Everyone at school seems to fit in except for me. Can you help me?"

"My friend Avery has autism and I think I might have it too. How can we find out if I am autistic?"

"I do not like big crowds or bright lights. Is there something wrong with me?"

How to Help Others With Autism

Never force someone to talk about their autism. If they choose to tell you, be a good listener. Do not question whether someone is actually autistic.

How each person experiences autism will be different. The best thing you can do is listen!

Lying under a weighted blanket can help during a meltdown.

Don't panic if someone has a meltdown. Let them stim and give them space. Never stop someone from stimming. If their stim is hurting them, find an adult who can help them find another way to stim.

the History of Autism

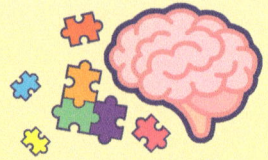

The word *autism* was first used in 1908. In 1938, Dr. Leo Kanner wrote about his young patients. They were very smart but had a "powerful desire for aloneness." He called their condition "early **infantile** autism." He pushed for adults to treat autistic children with kindness.

KEY WORD

Infantile: occurring in babies or young children.

In 1944, an Austrian doctor named Hans Asperger wrote about a milder form of autism. In 1981, many people with autism were diagnosed as having Asperger syndrome. Some people do not like the word Asperger's because Hans Asperger helped the German government during World War II. We do not diagnose people with Asperger's anymore.

The name Autism Spectrum Disorder (ASD) was first used in 2013. ASD includes all types of autistic people. Some people are starting to use the name Autism Spectrum Condition (ASC) because autism is not a disorder.

Autism Superheroes

Not everyone wants to talk about their autism. Do what feels comfortable for you and respect what other people decide. Here are some autism superheroes who are okay with sharing their experience having autism.

Hannah Gadsby was diagnosed with autism as an adult. She had always felt different and had trouble understanding social cues. The comedian loves connecting to a room of people and making them laugh.

Armani Williams was diagnosed with autism at two. He fell in love with auto racing as a kid and joined NASCAR when he was 16. Armani wants to inspire other people with autism to go after their dreams.

Greta Thunberg is known worldwide for her climate activism. Over four million people from 161 countries joined Greta in a climate strike. She calls her autism a 'superpower' and inspires many autistics.

Autism Tip 1: Self-Care

Taking care of your body can be hard if you are autistic. Strong smells or weird textures can be overwhelming. Find strategies that help you stay healthy!

Keep a sensory diary. It helps to know what sounds, feels or smells are hard for you. That way you can create a self-care routine just for you!

If the shower is too much, try taking a bath. If brushing your teeth is hard, try different kinds of toothbrushes. Also, try setting a timer! Knowing there is an end can help.

If something is hard to remember to do, make a schedule. Try putting a calendar on the fridge. Make it as detailed as you want and add rewards!

Autism Tip 2: Make Your Life Autism-Friendly

Every autistic person is different. Knowing what helps you is key to making your life autism-friendly!

Here are some ideas to make your life autism-friendly:

1. Make a safe space where you can get away.
2. Use stimming toys.
3. Set timers for things you do not like doing.
4. Give yourself time to enjoy your special interest.
5. Wear headphones to block out noise.
6. If you are going to a new place, do some research about it before you go.

Autism Tip 3:
Connect With Others

One out of 44 kids in the United States is autistic. That's around 1.7 million! Find other autistic kids near you or ask an adult to find virtual meetups.

Finding a community of people like you can be helpful and fun. You can make new friends and discover new things about yourself.

Quiz

Test your knowledge of autism by answering the following questions. The questions are based on what you have read in this book. The answers are listed on the bottom of the next page.

1 What part of the body does autism affect?

2 Is autism caused by medicine?

3 What is stimming?

4 What does non-verbal mean?

5 Name one autism superhero.

6 How many kids in the United States have autism?

Explore Other Level 3 Readers.

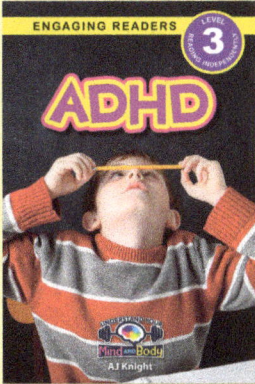

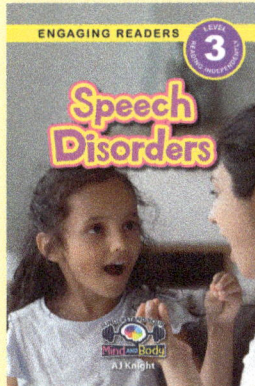

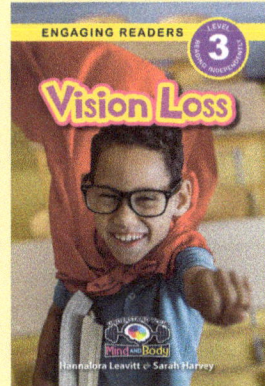

ENGAGING READERS — LEVEL 3
ADHD
AJ Knight

ENGAGING READERS — LEVEL 3
Anxiety
Adelaide Wilder

ENGAGING READERS — LEVEL 3
Asthma
Sarah Harvey

ENGAGING READERS — LEVEL 3
Body Image
Adelaide Wilder

ENGAGING READERS — LEVEL 3
Dyslexia
Sarah Harvey

ENGAGING READERS — LEVEL 3
Diabetes
Kit Caudron-Robinson

ENGAGING READERS — LEVEL 3
Obesity
Kit Caudron-Robinson

ENGAGING READERS — LEVEL 3
Speech Disorders
AJ Knight

ENGAGING READERS — LEVEL 3
Vision Loss
Hannalora Leavitt & Sarah Harvey

Visit www.engagebooks.com/readers

www.ingramcontent.com/pod-product-compliance
Lightning Source LLC
Chambersburg PA
CBHW040226040426
42331CB00039B/3371